Great Composers

Bach to Berlioz

Text by David Brownell   Art by Nancy Conkle

Domenico Scarlatti

ISBN 0-88288-058-X

GEORG PHILIPP TELEMANN
March 14, 1681 — June 25, 1767

During his long, productive life Georg Philipp Telemann wrote three brief autobiographies, which give us the sort of detail about Telemann's early years we wish we had for Bach and Handel. Born in Magdeburg, Telemann was the son and grandson of ministers. When Georg was four, his father died, leaving his mother three children and some property. Georg, the youngest, picked up music on his own: "In little schools I learned the usual things such as reading, writing, the Catechism, and a bit of Latin; but eventually I took up the violin, flute and cittern, with which I amused the neighbors, without so much as knowing that such a thing as written notes existed in the world" (1739 autobiography).

Telemann's mother decided music took too much of his time, and banned it: "Music and instruments were whisked away, and with them half my very life. But my fire burned far too brightly, and lighted my way into the path of innocent disobedience, so that I spent many a night with pen in hand because I was forbidden it by day, and passed many an hour in lonely places with borrowed instruments" (1718 autobiography).

At 20, Georg was sent off to Leipzig University to study law and "leave music." Resolved to turn over a new leaf, he took along only one of his works, and no instruments. At Leipzig Georg discovered that his roommate was a passionate music-lover, and the room full of music and instruments; Georg acted as if he knew nothing of music. Every evening students dropped in to play, but even though Georg was more skillful than any, he said nothing. One day, however, his roommate discovered Telemann's setting of the Sixth Psalm and arranged for it to be played in the church — following which the city authorities commissioned him to write a new choir piece every two weeks.

Georg now knew he was destined to be a musician, returned to his mother the money she'd just sent him, explaining why he didn't need it, and requested (and received) her permission to go on with a life in music. He formed and led a *collegium musicum* of forty students, an organization that survived Telemann.

In 1705 Telemann went off to an appointment at the small court of Count Erdmann von Promnitz at Sorau in a German-ruled part of Poland. Here Telemann wrote much music in the newly popular French style — Louis XIV's court set the style for all Europe. More important, Telemann heard Polish folk music, which he found exciting "in its true barbaric beauty," a hundred years or so before the period in which most composers began to take folk music seriously.

In early 1707 Telemann left Sorau to avoid a war, and become concertmaster at Eisenach for the Duke's orchestra. He also married Amalie Louise Juliane Eberlin. In Eisenach Telemann became friends with Johann Bernhard Bach, through whom he met Johann Bernhard's admired cousin Johann Sebastian. Later Telemann became godfather to J.S. Bach's second son, Carl Philipp Emanuel.

But only fifteen months after his wedding, Telemann's wife died giving birth to their daughter. Grieving for her, Telemann moved on to Frankfurt, as Director of Municipal Music. His duties included leading the music in one church, improving the performances, writing more music, supervising musical instruction at the town school, and writing pieces for municipal occasions. Having "a nature which cannot bear idleness," Telemann wanted more to do. He took charge of music at a second church, accepted commissions from his former employer the Duke of Saxe-Eisenach, and became Director and Secretary of the local *collegium musicum*, running its finances, organizing celebrations and banquets, supervising its smoking club, and writing for and leading its weekly concerts.

Amidst all this, Telemann found time to remarry — unwisely: he later called his second wife Maria Catharina Textor "my whimpering helpmeet."

Other cities sought Telemann: with their offers he jockeyed Frankfurt into raising his salary. In 1721 he received an irresistible offer — to be Hamburg's Town Cantor.

Hamburg fully appreciated its great cantor, and was prepared to pay him well. The town raised his salary fifty percent when Leipzig offered to make him cantor. (J. S. Bach got the job as Leipzig's third choice.) In Hamburg Telemann made three times as much as his friend Bach did in Leipzig — as much money as the mayor of Leipzig.

In his last years, like Bach and Handel, Telemann began to lose his eyesight — the natural consequence of a life spent making small marks on paper in poor lighting.

Telemann died June 25, 1767, at eighty-six, after forty-six years as Cantor of Hamburg, and was succeeded by his very gifted godson C.P.E. Bach. Telemann seems to have been blessed with talents so great that from his earliest years people deferred to him; a lively personality that made people enjoy working with him; such an abundance of energy that he could always enjoy doing two or three full-time jobs at once; creativity which never faltered and flourished amidst interruption — he was probably the most prolific of all composers; and a gift for happiness.

JEAN-PHILIPPE RAMEAU
1683-1764

Rameau, one of music's rare late-bloomers, at forty had not yet achieved the security to marry. Ten years later he had won a wife and some reputation as a musical theorist and composer, mainly of keyboard music; but at fifty he began a new career and wrote works which made him the predominant musician in France.

Little is known about Jean-Philippe Rameau's youth. The seventh child of Jean Rameau, church organist at Dijon, was christened Sept. 25, 1683. He spent some learning time in Italy, went to Paris to listen to one of the great French organists of the age, then was organist here and there in France.

At thirty-nine Rameau went to Paris and published his *Traité de l'harmonie*, which won him a reputation as a musical theorist. He increased this reputation with the success of his *Nouveau Système de musique théorétique* in 1726, four years later. Rameau's prose style is murky: some may have mistaken incomprehensibility for profundity.

We don't know what Rameau did to make money in Paris, but in February 1726 he felt he could afford to marry Marie-Louise Mangot, the nineteen-year-old daughter of a musical family. Even though people who described Rameau's personality used words like "irritable" and "difficult," the marriage seems to have been happy, and the Rameaus had four children.

Rameau published some keyboard works, and competed for jobs as an organist, but what he really wanted was to win fame and fortune by composing music for the stage. However, librettists were reluctant to gamble on a middle-aged theoretician with no theatrical experience.

Rameau's break came in the time-honored way — he found a patron. Le Riche de la Pouplinière, a man of taste and artistic interests, was a tax-farmer — a man who paid the government a fixed sum in advance for the right to collect certain taxes. Anything he made above the sum he'd paid, he was free to keep. Tax farmers were among the wealthiest (and most hated) men in France.

Rameau and his wife lived in Le Riche's household, with Rameau conducting the financier's private orchestra. Through Le Riche Rameau met Voltaire: after a long flirtation failed to result in a libretto, Le Riche found him Abbé Pellégrin and produced their opera *Hippolyte et Aricie* first at his mansion in 1733. The work became a public success, winning forty performances, and was revived nine years later for forty more.

The story comes from Euripides by way of Seneca and Racine, but readers familiar with those bloodcurdling masterpieces will be surprised to learn that here gallant Jupiter and kindly Diana bring about a happy ending. Eighteenth century operas were paid for by monarchs and other wealthy people who preferred the triumph of reason over emotion and of order over disorder on stage to stories of inevitable doom.

Rameau's success enabled him to push forward with more stage works: among the best were *Les Indes galantes* (1735), *Castor et Pollux* (1737), *Dardanus* (1739), *Platée* (1745), and *Zoroastre* (1749). Even less than Handel's do these works resemble what we think of as operas. Many of them follow in Lully's footsteps (and like Lully's, were intended for court premieres).

All are mixed spectacles with great scenic effects, long dance interludes, and very little form. *Les Indes galantes*, for example, starts with a mythological prologue, and follows with acts set in Turkey, Peru, Persia, and North America. There tends not be much conflict, development of characterization, or dramatic action: but the music can be sumptuous.

Rameau's works won court favor, and he was awarded pensions. By 1754, Rameau could afford to live on his own. Inevitably, however, his predominance attracted envy. The French like to set up combats supposedly between schools of thought to clip the wings of artists who are too successful, and Rameau's success made him titular leader of a party in several of these intellectual catfights. First came the battle between the *Lullistes* and the *Ramistes:* the former argued that only Lully (an Italian) had written proper French opera — and whenever Rameau deviated from formulas derived by studying Lully's works, he was debasing French opera and being Italianate; the *Ramistes* headed by Campra and Voltaire argued that Lully was antiquated, and Rameau great. Rameau himself was too intelligent to be a *Ramiste:* he admired Lully's works.

In 1752, Pergolesi's sprightly comedy *La Serva Padrona* won a great success in Paris; the previous quarrel was absorbed by *"La Guerre des Bouffons"* — the Clown War. This time the parties were "the French" and "the Italians" — both groups, of course, made up of Parisians. The former Lullistes and Ramistes joined forces against the invaders. They fought for the value of simple comic operas against Rameau's massive works. Again, Rameau himself liked some of these new works.

Acquaintances described the old Rameau in these years of his fame and success. Tall and skinny, he was "more like a ghost than a man." Rameau died September 12, 1764, nearly eighty-one; his widow survived until 1785, prudently dying before the French Revolution could void her pension.

JEAN-PHILIPPE RAMEAU after Carmontelle, Chantilly

DOMENICO SCARLATTI after Velasco, c. 1738; Alpiarca

DOMENICO SCARLATTI
October 26, 1685 — July 23, 1757

Domenico Scarlatti started out life like Bach — as one of a large family of musicians. His father, Alessandro, was an overpowering figure — the leading operatic composer in Naples, eventually writing 114 operas and over 700 cantatas. Domenico, the sixth son, was slow to find his own identity; for some years he worked here and there in Italy, very much in his father's shadow.

But he found no individual style or reliable income. Domenico was best known as a keyboard virtuoso: he and Handel competed in Roman drawing room performances. Their audiences agreed that on the harpsichord each performed so wonderfully that no one could say who excelled. Scarlatti, however, declared that until he had heard Handel play the organ, he had had no conception of the power of the instrument. They became friends; in later years when Scarlatti mentioned Handel, he usually crossed himself in veneration.

A job with the Portuguese ambassador led in 1719 to Scarlatti's appointment as *mestre* of the royal chapel for King João V in Lisbon; as he left Italy, Domenico must have felt that with half his life over, he'd achieve nothing that would live, and was going into exile from all centers of culture. In fact, isolation fostered Scarlatti's individuality, and his real career began.

As well as his duties in the chapel, he was music instructor for Don Antonio, the king's younger brother, and for the king's daughter Maria Barbara. She was intelligent, she knew six languages and in music she had real talent; teaching her became the most interesting part of Scarlatti's job. She became a competent composer, a skilled performer, and a genuine lover of music. In January 1729 sixteen-year-old Maria Barbara married Crown Prince Fernando of Spain, and took Scarlatti along as part of her royal household.

Domenico and the wife of sixteen he'd acquired during a visit to Rome in 1728 — proof of having financial security at last — now travelled from palace to palace with the Spanish court. King Felipe V was prematurely aged, shrunken, and in a state of depression so severe he would neither bathe nor change his clothes for a year at a time. Usually he napped at 5 a.m., got up again, went back to bed at 10 a.m. and slept till 5 p.m. His courtiers had to conform to his hours.

Scarlatti was the private property of Fernando and Maria Barbara: he gave no performances beyond the court circle. The keyboard sonatas that Scarlatti wrote for this private audience are highly individual, exploring virtuoso techniques, and working through various musical ideas and problems. These sonatas are the works in which Scarlatti found his own voice, and about which posterity cares. Perhaps no composer other than his contemporary Rameau made so late a start in his assault on fame.

In 1739 Scarlatti's wife died, leaving him with five children. By now a Spanish composer, Don Domingo remarried a Spanish wife, Anastasia Maxarti Ximenes, by whom he had four more children.

In 1746 King Felipe V died, and Fernando became King. Scarlatti continued to turn out his masterful sonatas for Queen Maria Barbara. They were unknown in his native Italy, France, and Germany, but a visitor took sonatas home to England, where his reputation began to grow.

As time passed, the court aged sadly. The royal couple were childless: Fernando melancholy, Maria Barbara obese and asthmatic. Scarlatti himself was ill, frequently housebound. Among his last compositions was a *Salve Regina*. Sensibly, he died before his royal patroness: he died in 1757, she in 1758.

GIUSEPPE TARTINI
April 8, 1692 - February 26, 1770

Giuseppe Tartini was the most celebrated violinist of his age and equally famed as a teacher and theorist. His many sonatas and concertos technically advanced the style of Corelli and added a personal passion to Corelli's dignified calm. His well known 'Devil's Trill' he wrote after dreaming of bargaining his soul to the Devil who then played for him "a sonata of such exquisite beauty as surpassed the boldest flights of (his) imagination."

GIUSEPPE TARTINI from his bust in the
Archivio della capella Antoniana, in Padua

JOHANN SEBASTIAN BACH from an unknown engraver.

JOHANN SEBASTIAN BACH (1685-1750)

Truth is often less probable than fiction: the two greatest baroque composers in all Europe were born one month apart, within a hundred miles of each other. Both good German Protestants, they crossed paths a number of times in the course of their lives—both even refused to marry the same woman: but they never met. And their careers and their personalities were as different as possible.

The composers, of course, are Johann Sebastian Bach and George Frideric Handel. Bach was born March 23, 1685, in the town of Eisenach, into a family of musicians so large that it might as well have been a union. All the Bachs descended from old Veit, who had died in 1619: it seems as if most of his many descendents went into music. The Bachs all over Germany knew when a good job was open, recommended other Bachs for it, and found Bachs to succeed them when they left a job. The family even had annual reunions, where they all extemporized polyphonically on popular songs, rather like a jazz jam session.

In Eisenbach a Bach was the church organist, and Johann's father played a string instrument there, and was a town musician. Johann went to the Latin school, and was so quick that soon he passed his brother, who was 3 years older. He sang in the choir of the church. But when he was 9, his mother died; his father followed within a year.

Johann and his brother Jakob were taken in by their oldest brother, Johann Christoph, in the town of Ohrdruf. Johann was there 5 years, contributing his earnings as a singer to the struggling household. It is said that his brother was harsh, but Johann later dedicated works to him, and trained two of his sons in music, so evidently he bore no grudges. In school he continued to be brilliant, with his strongest interests Latin and Lutheran theology. He was a senior at 14, 4 years younger than his classmates. He kept up his interest in theology all his life, reading extensively.

At 15 he was ready to begin his career. He walked 200 miles to join the choir at Luneberg. When his voice broke, he stopped singing but remained as organist and instrumentalist. Bach became one of the great organ virtuosos of the age (Handel was another), and an expert on organ construction, frequently hired as a consultant to test a new organ before the builder was paid.

In 1702 he was ready to go to university, but had no money. The family union informed him that Arnstadt Neue Kirche had a new organ, and no organist. Bach auditioned, and the committee was so impressed they didn't want to hear anyone else. He was expected to play 2 hours Sundays, perform 2 hours Thursdays, play at the Monday service, and train a small choir—all this while going to school. As his church was the third in the town, he had the third best performers, and the hot-tempered Bach, who was always a perfectionist, let them know when their work was inferior. One night he was attacked with a stick in the street by Geyersbach, a bassoonist, whom he had called a *zippelfaggottist*—someone who makes a bassoon sound like a nanny-goat. Bach drew his sword and put some holes in Geyersbach's clothes before they were separated. The city council reproved him for being turbulent, and rebuked him for playing the organ too inventively—people were confused by his music. He offended them again by taking 4 weeks' leave to go 230 miles to hear the great Buxtehude play the organ. While there he was offered a chance to inherit Buxtehude's very good job if he married Buxtehude's daughter, who was older than he was. Being already in love with his second cousin Maria Barbara, who lived in Arnstadt—there were Bachs in every town in Germany, it seems—he turned the lady down. (Handel refused the same package.)

JOHANN SEBASTIAN BACH after E. Hamman.

Back in Arnstadt he was rebuked for doing too little, having previously been rebuked for doing too much; the council were also distressed that he had a strange maiden in the organ gallery with him—apparently he was playing while Barbara sang. Fed up with the Arnstadt council's limited salary and unlimited interference, Bach looked for a new job: when he auditioned in Muhlhausen, the judges hired him at once after his trial performance. A cousin inherited the Arnstadt job—at less than half Bach's salary.

Now 22, Bach was able to marry on his new salary. He played the organ at all services, built a music library, wrote music, and worked to fix the organ. Having gotten caught in a clerical feud, he moved on in 1698 to become court organist at Weimar, leaving a cousin as his successor.

In Weimar he wrote a new cantata a month for his employer, the Duke; occasionally he went on a tour in which he served as a consultant about a new organ, performed as a virtuoso, and heard famous organists play. He became friendly with Georg Philipp Telemann (1681-1767), Handel's lifelong correspondent, and tried several times to hear Handel play, but to his great regret, never heard him. In 1716 Bach became angry when the Duke promoted another man to be *Kapellmeister*, and decided to quit. You did not, however, simply leave a noble employer: you had to have his permission. The Duke refused to let Bach resign: Bach, always determined, insisted, and the Duke put him in jail for a month for "too stubbornly forcing the issue of his dismissal." Bach got his way in the end, as was his habit. He and his family—by now there were seven children, most of them musical—went to Cöthen, where he conducted for a music-loving prince for six years.

In 1720 Barbara Bach died suddenly, leaving 4 surviving children. Bach recovered from this loss, and a year and a half later married Anna Magdalena Wicken, a soprano of 20, the daughter of the court trumpeter. She was a real musician, and a good companion to Bach: together they had 13 children, of whom 6 survived.

In 1723 Bach moved to his final job—the musical director of the churches of Leipzig, a city famous for music, even in Germany, with a choir school that had been founded in 1212. Leipzig had tried to hire Telemann: one of the councilors said, when Telemann refused, "Since one cannot get the best for this position of cantor, one must be contented with the mediocre." Not everyone can make a remark stupid enough to be funny 250 years later.

Bach's contract stipulated that his church music was not to be "too theatrical"; he had to teach Latin and the catechism in the choir school; he had to promise not to leave town without the mayor's permission; and so on. He lived in the school building, and one week of every four he was school inspector, on duty from dawn to 8 p.m. responsible for maintaining discipline—this in addition to his responsibility for the musical programs of the town's churches, two of which had elaborate music, with Sunday main services lasting 4 hours. Since good German Protestant towns had no opera, the church offered the principal public entertainment: Bach was expected to write music for many of the services—a new cantata each Sunday and feast day, and special music for Easter and Christmas. Bach wrote nearly 300 cantatas.

The disadvantage of Bach's job was that he had 24 bosses, the city council and the ecclesiastical consistory, most of whom wanted to tell Bach what to do. Bach never took orders very well: he argued with the council as to which students should be admitted to the choir school. The councilors were concerned with giving scholarships to orphans and the children of their friends: Bach wanted good musicians. Some of the pupils he rated as "useless." As for the town's musicians, "Discretion forbids my speaking at all truthfully of their competence and musical knowledge."

George Frideric Handel

This was as close to tact as Bach ever came, and better than his comment that the organist of the university's church "would have done better as a cobbler." Not surprisingly, the councilors considered him difficult, and occasionally spoke out against him in meetings.

But Bach did not fight with everyone: he was evidently a very good teacher, and his sons and many of his pupils turned into very good musicians. In Bach's later years his eyesight failed—an occupational hazard for men who spent hours bent over music paper, reading and copying, in an age with poor artificial lighting, Bach boldly risked having an eye operation performed by a traveling quack, who later treated Handel's blindness equally unsuccessfully. He had a stroke after the operation, and died July 18, 1750. The council eulogized him half-heartedly, and did next to nothing for his widow. His works, which were considered quite old-fashioned by this time, were put on the shelf, and his music was hardly remembered for 50 years. Four of his sons, however, became good composers—Wilhelm Friedemann (1710-1784), the oldest, his father's favorite, who worked in Berlin; Carl Philipp Emmanuel (1714-1788), who worked for Frederick the Great, then in Hamburg; Johann Christoph Friedrich (1732-1795), who worked at Bückeburg; and Johann Christian (1735-1782), "the London Bach," who gave lessons to the child Mozart. The sons remembered their father's music, and occasionally played it for others. C. P. E. transmitted some of Bach's music to Baron Gottfried van Swieten of Vienna, who made it known to Haydn, Mozart, and Beethoven. As other composers came to know Bach's "old-fashioned" music, they fell under the spell of its incredible craftsmanship, and the joy of music written for "the glory of God and the recreation of the soul."

GEORGE FRIDERIC HANDEL (1685-1759)

George Frideric Handel was born February 23, 1685 in Halle. His family, unlike Bach's, was not musical, but George learned to play keyboard instruments. When George was eight, the ruling Duke heard him play and told his father that it would be criminal not to foster such a talent. Dr. Handel, the Duke's physician, felt that a musical career would be a step down socially, but grudgingly turned his son over to the Halle organist, Friedrich Wilhelm Zachow, a good organist, composer and teacher. By 11 George could substitute for Zachow in church performances and had begun composing. Handel remained friendly with Zachow, and later in his career sent money to aid Zachow's widow.

In 1697 Dr. Handel died; George followed his plans and went to Halle University to study philosophy and law. But his goal was still a career in music. In 1702, still a student, Handel became probationary organist at Halle Cathedral, even though he was Lutheran and it was Calvinist. At the end of his trial year, he was offered the job—a good start for a career like Bach's.

But Handel did not want to work in the small rigid world of German Protestantism. He turned the job down and went off to Hamburg—the nearest city where he could work with opera.

Hamburg was one of the most cosmopolitan German cities; Handel spent 3 years there, starting as a violinist for the opera orchestra. He became the inseparable companion of Johann Mattheson (1681-1764), who was beginning his career as a singer, harpsichordist, organist, and composer; later in life he also became an important critic and writer on music. Mattheson quickly recognized that the quiet young Saxon had talent. At this stage of his life Handel apparently enjoyed putting

GEORGE FRIDERIC HANDEL, The Charming Brute, after an engraving by Joseph Goupy, 1754.

people on: Mattheson later reminisced, "He acted as though he didn't know how many beans make five. I know well how he will laugh up his sleeve when he reads this, although he laughs outwardly but little." In later years, Handel's friends record, he often told jokes—something one can't imagine Bach doing—but not everyone could follow his jokes, as he used a combination of English, German, French and Italian, selecting whatever word was handiest.

In 1705 Handel's first opera, *Almira*, was performed successfully in Hamburg, with Mattheson singing the lead. Handel immediately composed another: all his life, even in an age of quick and prolific composers, Handel was incredibly productive. Meanwhile Mattheson's opera *Cleopatra* was a success, with Mattheson singing Antony, and Handel conducting from the harpsichord. One performance, after Mattheson had died on stage, he came into the pit and wanted to take over conducting for the last part of the act, to demonstrate his versatility. Handel refused to yield his place. The two quarrelled, and the opera ended with them going off to the Goosemarket, followed by much of the audience, and having at each other with their swords. Mattheson later recalled, "The duel might have ended very badly for us both if by God's mercy my sword had not broken on a metal button of my adversary's coat. . . . We became better friends than ever." They remained correspondents all Handel's life.

Even though Handel had been sending money home to his mother, he managed to save enough in Hamburg to finance his next venture—a trip to Italy, still the operatic center of the world. Like Bach, Handel had a passion to hear what other musicians were doing; but Handel's desire took him beyond Germany. From 1706 to 1710 he learned all that he could from the Italian musicians. He became particularly friendly with Domenico Scarlatti (1685-1757), a shy virtuoso, as good on the harpsichord as Handel himself. Handel learned Italian, wrote several successful operas, and seems to have had a love affair or two. Although Handel was the first composer who was regarded as important enough to deserve a biography, we know very little about his personal life: he was a private man and kept his secrets. Still, his biographer in 1760 says of a Florentine singer, La Bombace, "Handel's youth and comeliness, joined with his fame and abilities in Music, had made impressions on her heart." In his later years, however, it seems as if Handel decided that he could work best in solitude, and chose to live a life in which love was not important.

Despite his various successes in Italy, Handel chose to leave. Perhaps he disliked being pressed to become Catholic: he later told an English friend that he liked England because there a man's religious views were his own business. A job as court composer for the Elector of Hanover gave him a secure foothold from which to pay his first visit to England, in 1710. After a success with an opera, he touched base in Hanover with his employer, using his spare time to study English, and returned permanently to England in October, 1712. He returned occasionally to the Continent to recruit singers, and visit his mother: but England became his home, and he became an Englishman.

From 1723 on he lived happily and comfortably in his house on Lower Brook Street. He collected paintings, owning two by Rembrandt, and was very fond of a good dinner: eventually he became rather stout, and the object of caricatures. Dr. Burney, the musicologist, who knew him, says Handel was large and unwieldy, and generally looked "heavy and sour: but when he *did* smile, it was his sire the sun bursting out of a black cloud. . . . He was impetuous, rough, and peremptory in his manners and conversation, but totally devoid of ill-nature or malevolence."

Handel's profession was enough to make a man both sour and peremptory: the world of eighteenth-century opera was a strange one, and he had to fight many battles in order to survive in it. Opera singers were egocentric, and refused to tolerate rivals: at one point in a Handel opera, two sopranos, Bordoni and Cuzzoni, each supported by her own faction, and enraged by the opposition's catcalls, engaged in a hair-pulling fight on stage. Singers also added freely to the music to show off their voices, to the great annoyance of Handel, who, like Bach, cared passionately that his music be performed correctly: his biographer records that once he seized Cuzzoni "by the waist, and if she made any more words, swore that he would fling her out of the window." The highly paid singers also would go over to an opposing manager if they got a better offer. Theatre owners could also be a problem: Owen Swiney ran off to Italy with the box office takings from one successful opera before anyone got paid. Political quarrels sometimes led to the establishing of rival opera companies, which imported other composers to ruin Handel. And anyone who disliked him accused him of being a foreigner: when his company went to Oxford, one Jacobite professor complained that the university was profaned by the presence of "one Handel, a forreigner, and his lowsy crew of forreign Fiddlers."

Sometimes Handel's operas were great, sometimes inferior; sometimes he made fortunes, sometimes he was nearly bankrupt: but always he fought bravely—like Bach, he was a fighter—and always he dealt honestly. Once he had to advertise in the newspapers that patrons who had subscribed for his opera's season should come to his house to be paid back for the remainder of the season: he could perform no more, as he was losing too much money. A patron wrote the papers to suggest Handel's subscribers should refuse to demand their refunds, to aid Handel. Most did refuse: Handel thereupon announced he would continue performing, to meet his obligation and repay this gesture of confidence, "Let the *Risque* which I may run be what it will."

Nothing defeated him: in 1737, he suffered a major stroke and seemed to be at the end of his career, but with characteristic determination he regained control over his body and mind, and was soon hard at work again. He began setting English texts instead of Italian, and produced oratorios instead of operas. "As I perceived, that joining good Sense and significant Words to Musick, was the best Method of recommending Musick to an English Audience; I have directed my Studies that way, and endeavour'd to show, that the English Language, which is so expressive of the sublimest Sentiments is the best adapted of any to the full and solemn Kind of Musick."

With the passage of time he became England's national composer. What Dr. Burney called "Handel's big Bow-Wow manner" was recognized as the only appropriate accompaniment for ceremonial state occasions, such as coronations, and he was revered by his public. One Englishman who met Handel recorded in his diary that he had just met "a man of the vastest genius and skill in music that perhaps has lived since Orpheus."

He continued hard at work, producing two oratorios a year until, like Bach, he was disabled by blindness. The score of his last oratorio *Jeptha* records the progress of his blindness in marginal notes: "got so far as this on Wed. Feb. 13, 1751, unable to continue because of the weakening of the sight of my left eye" (the right was already blind). He was able to finish, and continued bravely, with no complaints. In a letter of about this period to his old friend Telemann he asks after Telemann's health, sends him some plants (Telemann was a passionate gardener), and says nothing of his own blindness. He was not a man given to complaining.

In his last years Handel occasionally dictated new arias for the oratorios he revived: he continued to lead them, as well as improvising on the organ at intermissions. He continued his annual performances of *The Messiah* for the benefit of the Royal Foundling Hospital, of which he was a governor, and which inherited his score on his death. During the April 6 performance of *The Messiah* in 1759, Handel fainted. He was taken home, and died there April 14. His burial in Westminster Abbey was a public occasion, attended by three thousand people.

Unlike Bach, Handel left no children: but his works made all subsequent musicians his heirs. Gluck hung Handel's portrait on his wall, to be the first thing he saw in the morning; Mozart said, "When he chooses, he strikes like thunder." Haydn commented, "Here is the master of us all," and one of the great joys of Beethoven's last days was his receiving a gift of an edition of Handel. "He is the greatest of us all," he said: "I can still learn from him."

CHRISTOPH WILLIBALD GLUCK (1714-1787)

Born July 2, 1714 in Erasbach, the son of a forester for Prince Lobkowitz, Christoph Willibald Gluck ended his life as the Chevalier Gluck, Royal and Imperial Court Composer to the Holy Roman Emperor, and a well-to-do international celebrity—all of which goes to show what success in the world of opera could do for a poor boy. In the process of succeeding Gluck also reformed opera.

We know little about Gluck's youth: he was brought up in music-loving Bohemia, played violin and cello in Prague, where he may have gone to university, then went to Vienna to play chamber music as one of Prince Lobkowitz's musicians. He moved on to Italy, studying further in Milan with Giovanni Battista Sammartini (1698-1775). There he wrote his first opera *Artaserse*, a success in 1741.

This and the nine other Italian operas Gluck wrote over the next three and a half years, most of which are now lost, were very much standard baroque operas. Several had librettos by Pietro Metastasio (1698-1782), the Imperial court poet and dramatist, whose immensely popular 27 librettos were used again and again. *Artaserse* was set 40 times over a hundred years; some composers even set the same Metastasio libretto several times. Handel, Gluck, Haydn, Mozart, Hasse, Piccini, and many other composers set Metastasio's works. Their plots are intricate, but tidy: A loves B, who loves C instead, while C loves D, who is in love with A. A uses D's jealousy of B to entangle her in a political conspiracy. Everyone declaims in a flowery way about his emotions; each singer gets a show-off rejected love aria, jealousy aria, and triumphant love aria. Nobody does anything, nothing happens, and at the opera's end no one's feelings are hurt. Gluck's works fit into this tradition and offered Italian audiences no surprises or difficulties, other than that of pronouncing the composer's German name: they called him "Klug."

After leaving Italy Gluck traveled to London in 1745 with Prince Lobkowitz. He was now a musical wanderer, writing and conducting Italian operas all over Europe. In London he wrote a couple of unsuccessful operas, and gave a concert with Handel, playing his "concerto upon 16 drinking-glasses tuned with spring water." Back in Germany he wrote music to celebrate several royal weddings and impressed the Empress Maria Theresa. He toured Germany and Denmark; sometimes his operas succeeded, sometimes they failed.

Gluck's life changed in September, 1750, when he married Marianne Pergin, the daughter of a rich merchant. Hereafter he had enough money to be able to do as he chose. He continued writing operas for various cities—Prague, Naples—where he was

CHRISTOPH WILLIBALD GLUCK after the painting by Duplessis; Vienna.

known by different variants of his name—Gluckh, Cluch, "il famoso Kluk"—but he refused to compromise his artistic standards. In Vienna in 1754 he was made court *Kapellmeister.* In 1756 the Pope gave him a knighthood, making him "the Chevalier Gluck," a helpful title in a rank-conscious age.

But Gluck's best works came after all these successes, later in life than usual for composers. The experience he gained through writing many operas had given him ideas about what opera should be, and with the aid of two men with similar theories, he was able to put his ideas on stage. The director of the court theatres, Count Durazzo, and Durazzo's friend the poet Ranieri da Calzabigi (1714-1795), a friend of Casanova's of similar habits, joined with Gluck to attack Metastasian opera. Calzabigi wrote, "Gluck hated these meek political, philosophical, and moral views of Metastasio's, his metaphors, his garrulous passions, his geometrically devised word-plays. Gluck liked emotions captured from simple nature, mighty passions at boiling point and at the climax of their outbreak, loud theatrical tumults."

Calzabigi's libretto for their first opera together, *Orfeo ed Euridice,* performed October 5, 1762, returned to Monteverdi's original subject and brought genuine emotion and simplicity back to opera. They followed up with *Alceste* in 1767: Calzabigi's librettos, Gluck wrote, "are full of those well-managed situations, those terrible and pathetic features, which hold out to the composer the means of expressing great passions and creating energetic and touching music. However much soever of talent a composer may have, he will never produce any but mediocre music if the poet does not awaken in him that enthusiasm without which the productions of all the arts are but feeble and drooping."

After a scandal had led to Calzabigi's departure from Vienna, Gluck decided to take his new operas to Paris. There the German composer who had written Italian operas all over Europe reformed French opera by writing operas in French. He faced a good deal of opposition from French musicians, partly as an outsider, partly because he was a tough, outspoken man who rudely demanded a great deal from his musicians. Gluck conducted his own operas to prevent others from mishandling them. He demanded enough time and enough rehearsals to prepare his operas properly, and would refuse to have them performed if he did not get what he wanted. In Paris he was aided by his former pupil, Queen Marie Antoinette, who backed up "M. Glouch," as the French called him, in his demands.

Rehearsals with Gluck were painful. His sensitive ears were outraged by the errors of singers and musicians: he would scream, "This isn't worth a hoot in hell!" at the offenders. Gluck once said that if he got 20 livres for composing an opera, he should be paid 20,000 for enduring its rehearsals.

In private life he was calmer. A hearty eater and drinker, inclined to overindulge, he and his wife were happily married. Childless, in 1769 they adopted Marianne, Mme. Gluck's ten-year-old niece. The great sorrow of their life was her death of smallpox in 1776. "How lonely I shall be from now on!" he wrote.

After the success of his first French opera, *Iphigene en Aulide* in April 1774, and of his French revision of *Orfeo,* he produced operas in Paris, returning to Vienna for comfort. As he aged, he regretted having spent his life composing in other languages. "I have now grown very old, and have squandered the best powers of my mind upon the French nation, regardless of which I feel an inward impulse to make something for my own nation yet." He worked on a German text, but he composed in his head, never writing his music down until he had finished thinking it out. A series of small strokes and a bad stroke in 1781 ended his composing before his German project was written down. Gluck lived on until November, 1787, when a final stroke came after he had had more wine than his doctor allowed him.

FRANZ JOSEPH HAYDN in the Esterhazy uniform, after Grundmann; 1768.

FRANZ JOSEPH HAYDN (1732-1809)

If one could choose to have been a particular composer, I would choose Haydn. No one goes through life without grief and pain, and Haydn had at least his share; but he was blessed with the gift of cheerfulness, and during the last thirty years of his long productive life had the great pleasure of turning out one masterwork after another.

His life was not easy. Born March 31, 1732 at Rohrau, on the border of Austria and Bohemia, he was the eldest son of a wheelwright. His mother cooked at the local manor. Father Matthias loved folk songs and played the harp; Joseph quickly picked up some musical knowledge and was singing by the age of five. A relative who kept a school took Haydn there, and taught him music. Joseph survived the school, "even though I got more floggings than food," and after two years was heard by the choirmaster of St. Stephen's Cathedral in Vienna, who was touring the countryside to find boys with good voices. Impressed by Joseph's quickness and intelligence, he took the eight-year-old back to Vienna, a city Haydn loved all his life.

Despite being poorly taught, the small, ragged, underfed boy picked up a knowledge of music. His brother Michael came to join the choir: he too became a composer later. In 1745 Haydn's voice broke; in 1749, after a prank, he was turned out of the choir to find a place for himself in the world.

In doing so Haydn had to survive several very hard years. Penniless, he lived in an attic with a leaky roof, where he had a worm-eaten harpsichord. He worked from dawn till late at night, teaching, composing, playing the violin with street musicians, and practicing new pieces. He particularly liked the keyboard sonatas of C.P.E. Bach: "I didn't leave the clavier until I had mastered them all. I played them many times for my own delight, especially when I felt oppressed and discouraged."

In 1758 his luck changed: he got a job as *kapellmeister* for a nobleman, leading an orchestra of 16. Financially secure, Haydn decided to marry. He loved his pupil Therese Keller, the daughter of a barber who had helped Haydn in his lean years, but Therese decided to become a nun; so Haydn married her older sister Maria. Haydn's common sense, which usually protected him, failed on this occasion: Maria was a foolish, ill-tempered shrew, ugly and extravagant, who disliked music. Haydn found little pleasure in his marriage, but occasionally discovered consolation elsewhere.

In 1761 Haydn was hired as assistant *kapellmeister* by the Esterhazy family, for whom he was to work for 32 years. These fabulously wealthy Hungarian nobles maintained one of the best musical establishments in Europe. As a servant of Prince Esterhazy, Haydn wore his master's uniform, and reported for orders twice a day. He had to select and manage an orchestra of about 20 (the musicians loved him, and called him "Papa"), conduct them in two two-hour concerts a week, assemble and organize a music library, copy music, and compose pieces for them to play. Evidently he worked long hours: on one of his scores, he mixed up the staves in different parts, then corrected his error, adding the note, "Written while asleep."

His Prince liked to play the baryton, an old-fashioned knee viol, so Haydn wrote about 200 baryton pieces for him. Esterhaza Palace had an opera theatre, seating 400, so Haydn wrote 23 operas. One season he supervised the production of 17 operas, for 125 performances. By the time he ceased composing, Haydn had piled up 4 oratorios, 104 symphonies, 83 string quartets, 52 piano sonatas, 14 masses, and a great many other works in every form requested of him.

Working at Esterhaza had its drawbacks. Sometimes the musicians (Haydn's contract forbade him to socialize with them) were surly because the palace had too little room for their wives to live there. Often Haydn missed the gaiety of Vienna's social life, and regretted living in the middle of a Hungarian swamp, without a chance to exchange ideas with other musicians. But, on the whole, he felt he had been fortunate: "My Prince was always satisfied with my work. Not only did I have the encouragement of constant approval, but as conductor of the orchestra I could experiment, find out what made a good effect, and what weakened it, so I was free to alter, improve, add, or omit, and be as bold as I pleased. Cut off from the world I had no one to bother me and I was forced to become original."

Haydn's fame soon spread beyond Esterhaza, but Haydn was always modest about his talents. He always attributed most of his success to hard work, and said, "Young people can learn from my example that something can come out of nothing. What I have become is all the result of dire need." He was forced, however, to admit, "I did, of course, have talent." "I was never a quick writer," he said, "and composed with care and diligence."

Unlike many other composers, Haydn was never jealous of his fellows. He freely admitted Mozart was his superior: "My friends often flatter me about my talent," he said, "but he was far above me." He took pleasure in telling Mozart's father, "Before God and as an honest man, I tell you that your son is the greatest composer known to me, either in person or by name." Haydn and Mozart genuinely liked each other, and each learned from the other. We have a letter Haydn wrote a Prague theatre manager, declining to send him an opera to compete with Mozart's there: "the *great Mozart* can scarcely have his equal. For if I were able to impress the soul of every music-lover, and more especially the great ones, with my own understanding of and feeling for Mozart's incomparable works, *so profound* and so full of *musical intelligence*, as my own *strong sentiment* dictates, then the nations would vie with each other to possess such a jewel within their boundaries. Let Prague hold fast to the precious man—but also reward him; for without that the story of great genius is a sad one and gives posterity little encouragement for further effort; for which reason, alas, so many hopeful spirits suffer defeat. It makes me angry to think that this *unique* Mozart has not yet found an appointment at some imperial or royal court! Forgive me if I stray from my subject. I love the man too much..."

It was in his later years that Haydn came to know Mozart. In 1790 his Prince died, and the successor pensioned Haydn off. He went to live in his beloved Vienna. Johann Peter Saloman, an impresario, offered him a contract to travel to England, a country mad about good music, but without a native great composer. Going there was an adventure for a man of 58, and Mozart tried to dissuade Haydn from going to a place where he did not know the language: "My language is understood all over the world," Haydn answered. At a farewell luncheon given Haydn by his friends, Mozart embraced him, and the two wept. Mozart said, "We shall not see each other ever again," and he was correct; but he, not Haydn, died, to Haydn's shock.

Haydn arrived in England January 1, 1791, to an enthusiastic welcome. Oxford gave him a doctorate, an attractive widow gave him her heart, and the public gave him their money. Haydn called these the happiest years of his life, and returned wealthy. In the course of two visits Haydn composed his last 12 symphonies, and was asked by King George III to remain; but a new Esterhazy Prince wanted him to come home to Vienna, and write one mass a year. In these last years Haydn wrote his two great oratorios and six of his masses. Uncharacteristically he admitted, "I am rather proud of my masses." He had reason to be. It was of the masses Haydn also said, "Since God has given me a cheerful heart, He will forgive me for serving Him cheerfully."

We have a letter to his publisher from 1799, telling us about his composing in this period: "Unfortunately my affairs multiply with my years, *and yet it is almost as if with the decrease in my spiritual powers, my desire and the urgency to work increase. O God, how much is still to be done in this splendid art, even by such a man as I have been!* The world, to be sure, compliments me many times a day, even on the fire of my last works; no one, however, will believe with what toil and exertion I have to search it out, while on many a day my weak memory and flagging nerves so wear me down that I sink into the dreariest state and am thus in no condition for many days afterwards to find even a single idea, until finally, encouraged by Providence, I can sit down again at the clavier and there begin to hammer away. *Then everything is all right again, God be praised!* "

After 1802 Haydn composed little, but lived comfortably in Vienna, honored by all. His death came May 31, 1809; his last words are supposed to have been, "Children, be comforted, I am well."

WOLFGANG AMADEUS MOZART (1756-1791)

Mozart's fate shows how fortunate Haydn was in having such intelligent patrons as the Esterhazys. A composer needed a reliable source of income to survive, as Wolfgang's father Leopold was always telling him.

In many ways a child prodigy could hardly have found a better father than Leopold Mozart. A musician and a composer, Leopold provided a musical background for baby Wolfgang (who was born in Salzburg, January 17, 1756), recognized the early indications of his musical talent, and gave him lessons early. Wolfgang watched papa teach older sister Marianne ("Nannerl") when she was seven, and begged for lessons too. He started at four.

Leopold realized that his son was miraculously talented, and described him as "this marvel of nature, placed in the world by God." He trained the boy well, disciplined him, and taught him to make his manuscripts tidy. He wrote down Wolfgang's first compositions, since the boy was too young to write legibly yet, and tried to advance Wolfgang's interests by taking him about Europe, so that he could hear the music of many composers, become known by displaying his talents, and perhaps earn a lot of money for himself and the family.

When Wolfgang was 6, the family went to Munich; next year Wolferl and Nannerl played in Vienna for the Empress Maria Theresa, who let Wolferl climb into her lap and kiss her. They were admired, but they did not become rich. In 1763, in spite of the displeasure of Leopold's employer, the Archbishop of Salzburg, who wanted his assistant *kapellmeister* to stay home and work, they were off again. In Mannheim they heard the greatest orchestra of the period, and Wolfgang was overwhelmed to hear what orchestral playing could be. In Paris he and Nannerl played for the royal family, and he wrote his first published works—4 piano sonatas—wearing a pinafore to help keep ink off his clothes. In London, Wolfgang, now 8, wrote his first 4 symphonies, and took some lessons from J.C. Bach. Daines Barrington, an amateur scientist, came to find out whether Wolfgang was as talented and as young as was claimed: "whilst he was playing to me, a favorite cat came in, on which he left his harpsichord, nor could we bring him back for a considerable time." Despite his genius, Wolfgang was still a child!

The Mozarts, no richer than before, had to return to Salzburg after three and a half years. When a stingy and mean-spirited new Archbishop took the throne in

MOZART when he was six,
after an unknown artist.
Mozart-Museum,
Salzburg.

Salzburg, he objected to the Mozarts making efforts to get jobs elsewhere, or traveling, but gave his own best jobs to Italian musicians. When Wolfgang was 21, Leopold decided he must find a good position. The Archbishop refused to grant them leave, so Wolfgang quit, and Leopold sent him off with mama to take care of him.

Perhaps Leopold had been too good a father: Wolfgang had never had to plan for himself, and never got to be good at the practical jobs papa had done—publicizing himself, being polite to powerful but tasteless people, planning ahead, budgeting. Like many prodigies, he remained immature in many ways outside his own profession. He infuriated Leopold by his fecklessness, and the way in which he preferred making music to making a career.

The first place he went on this important tour was Mannheim, to hear that marvellous orchestra again. And the first thing he did there was to fall in love with Aloysia Weber, the daughter of a poor copyist, prompter, and singer—not at all the sort of girl papa wanted for him. Aloysia was only 15, but had a splendid voice, not yet trained: Mozart wanted to stay there and help her become a great opera singer. Papa wrote him a ten-page letter of protest: you are too ready to let others make use of you; you must go to Paris and find a place in the world.

Paris was a disaster: The Parisians did not care about another young piano virtuoso. A friend wrote papa, "He is too *sincere,* not active enough, too susceptible to illusions, too little aware of the means of achieving success. Here in order to succeed, one must be artful, enterprising, and bold." The short, rather ugly Mozart didn't impress people, and he had a talent for making enemies by casually dismissing as negligible the music of lesser composers—which was.

Worse followed: mama fell sick, and despite Mozart's nursing, died July 3, 1778. He tried to break the news gently to papa and Nannerl. On his way back to Salzburg, when he stopped to see Aloysia, she had no use for him: she had taken the short cut to success of becoming a nobleman's mistress.

He returned to Salzburg with confused and tired emotions, took a job as organist with the Archbishop, and kept composing. In 1781 the Archbishop took him along to Vienna, but wouldn't use him, or let him play for others. They quarreled and Mozart quit, his parting speeded by a kick in the rump from his offensive employer's secretary. He went off to lodge with his friends the Webers, and became interested in Aloysia's younger sister Constanze. Despite Papa's strong opposition he married her in 1782.

Constanze was cheerful and affectionate, but scatter-brained and no more economical than Wolfgang, who was always ready to spend money he didn't have on something he really wanted, such as "that beautiful red coat which took my fancy so vastly." They lived together happily, always with a pet—Mozart loved dogs, cats, and birds. On Sunday mornings they gave quartet parties. Mozart became friendly with Haydn, and wrote six quartets dedicated to him—"It was from Haydn that I learned to write quartets," he explained. Otherwise he worked busily, either writing music or playing it, so that his fingers were often cramped. For exercise he would go off to play bowls or billiards with friends. For money he would organize a concert and write a new concerto for it. He was perhaps the greatest pianist in Europe. If he did not finish writing out the concerto in time, he would play his part from memory, with a blank sheet of paper in front of him.

We have a letter in which Mozart talks about how he composed. "When I am . . . completely myself, entirely alone, and of good cheer—say, traveling in a carriage, or walking after a good meal, or during the night, when I cannot sleep—. . . on such occasions my ideas flow best and most abundantly. *Whence* and *how* they come, I know not; nor can I force them. Those ideas that please me I retain in memory, and am accustomed, as I have been told, to hum them to myself. If I continue in this way, it soon occurs to me how I may turn this or that morsel to account, so as to make a good dish of it, that is to say, agreeably to the rules of counterpoint, to the peculiarities of the various instruments, etc.

All this fires my soul, and, provided I am not disturbed, my subject enlarges itself, becomes methodized and defined, and the whole, though it be long, stands almost complete and finished in my mind, so that I can survey it, like a fine picture or a beautiful statue, at a glance. Nor do I hear in my imagination the parts *successively*, but I hear them, as it were, all at once. What a delight this is I cannot tell! All this inventing, this producing, takes place in a pleasing lively dream. Still, the actual hearing of the *tout ensemble* is after all the best. What has been thus produced I do not easily forget, and this is perhaps the best gift I have my divine maker to thank for."

After having a composition completed in his mind, Mozart could write it down quickly, while talking with people around him. He even wrote one piece while sitting by Constanze, who was in labor.

All his brilliance did not bring him what he really wanted in Vienna—the chance to write operas. The chief Court Composer Antonio Salieri had no intention of sharing his advantages with others, and he had control of musical patronage. But a new friend, the new Court Opera Poet, the engaging Venetian ex-priest Lorenzo Da Ponte (1749-1838), who had all the political skills Mozart lacked, provided the opportunity Mozart wanted. They made an opera out of the new French comedy, *The Marriage of Figaro*. "As fast as I wrote the words, he set them to music." Da Ponte outmaneuvered rival composers, and protected the opera from the intrigues of the Italian singers, and it succeeded.

In Prague it played steadily for nearly six months, after the Viennese had forgotten it; the manager of the local opera, which had been saved from bankruptcy by its success, commissioned Mozart and Da Ponte to write him another. Da Ponte was working on three librettos at once, sustained by a decanter of Tokay, a box of snuff, and a sixteen-year-old girl who came whenever he rang.

Mozart took the libretto for *Don Giovanni* to Prague, and worked busily composing, but the overture was not yet written down the night before the premiere, October 19, 1787. He sat up most of the night, with Constanze telling him fairy stories to keep him awake. The orchestra parts came to the theatre from the copyist twenty minutes late, and the orchestra played an overture it had never seen. "A good many notes fell under the desks, to be sure," said Mozart, "but it went off quite well, just the same." The opera triumphed: "My Praguers understand me," he said.

But back in Vienna matters went poorly. Constanze was often ill, and debts increased faster than they could be paid. A new emperor fired Da Ponte in 1790, and he went off to London. Mozart wrote desperately for money; bill collectors hounded him. His fellow-Mason Michael Puchberg generously loaned him money whenever Mozart asked, but this was not enough. Mozart worked very hard setting a German libretto written by Emmanuel Schikaneder, a shady entrepreneur who ran a theatre for common people in a wooden shack in the suburbs.

Mozart's health began to fail with fatigue. A gaunt stranger appeared and commissioned him to write a requiem mass, but refused to give his name. Mozart saw this as a visit from death, and believed the requiem would be for himself.

The Magic Flute opened successfully. Mozart was increasingly ill, fainting and having severe headaches, but he hung about backstage during performances to hear the audience love his opera. He kept working on the *Requiem:* "Here is my deathsong; I must not leave it incomplete."

Soon he could no longer leave his bed; they took away the *Requiem* score to keep him from working on it. He would look at his watch in the evening, to hear in his mind the aria of *The Magic Flute* that was sung at that point. The day before he died his friends came and sang for him the parts of the *Requiem* which were finished, so he could hear it.

He died December 5, 1791 of kidney disease, nervous exhaustion, and malnutrition. He was given a pauper's funeral in a storm; his grave is lost. The Emperor gave his widow a pension for life—about $10 a month.

If Mozart had lived twice as long—as long as Haydn—he would have heard all Beethoven's works, and what other composers wrote up to the early works of Berlioz. Who can begin to guess what he would have written?

LUDWIG VAN BEETHOVEN (1770-1827)

Beethoven was one of those rare men whose contemporaries quickly realize that they are great. Mozart heard him play as a teenager, and said, "He will make a noise in the world some day." Haydn recommended young Beethoven for a job, saying, "Beethoven will in time fill the position of one of Europe's greatest composers." People kept notes of their meetings with Beethoven, knowing that posterity would be interested. In his own lifetime he was recognized as the greatest living musician: when he died, between fifteen and twenty thousand Viennese came to honor him as his body was taken to the cemetery.

I suppose that even in the musical city of Vienna, where citizens were willing to sign a petition urging Beethoven not to disgrace the city by allowing any place else to have the premieres of his new Ninth Symphony and Missa Solemnis, there were not twenty thousand people who understood his music. Perhaps what they recognized in him was the personality which is reflected in the music, with its great strength and power to win tremendous battles. People writing about Beethoven compared him to a lion or a bear.

Beethoven's life was always a struggle. He was born December 16, 1770, in the small city of Bonn, where his grandfather and his father were both musicians for the reigning Elector. Grandfather was a bass singer and *kapellmeister*—a successful man whose portrait Ludwig kept and prized all his life. Father was a singer—an inventory of the Elector's musicians describes him as having "a rather stale voice"—and gave music lessons. He quickly recognized his son's musical talents, and trained him, hoping to make money, as Leopold Mozart had. But Johann van Beethoven lacked Leopold Mozart's showmanship, and Ludwig lacked Wolfgang's charm. Local well-to-do music lovers gave him financial help, cultural training, and friendship. When he was seventeen, they sent him to Vienna for further training. He went to Mozart for lessons, but within two weeks the news that his mother was dying called him back to Bonn. After her death Ludwig's father fell apart. He took to drink, and his salary had to be given to his son so that his family could survive. Ludwig became responsible for his two brothers.

In 1792 a grant from the Elector helped him return to Vienna, where he remained for the rest of his life. He took a few lessons from Haydn, who recom-

Missa Solemnis
Op. 123

After Josef Stieler, 1819.

mended him for jobs. Although his teachers described him as "headstrong," they recognized that he was a fine pianist and perhaps the greatest improviser of the age. Local music-lovers appreciated his talents and aided him: he spent two years living in the home of Prince Lichnowsky, a Viennese music-lover who was to be a generous patron all his life.

As a composer Beethoven developed slowly. He was not ready to publish an Opus One until 1794, when he was 24. He said that musical ideas came to him continuously, but he worked them over for a long time before being satisfied. His memory, he said, was so good that he never forgot an idea. We have some of his notebooks and scores, which offer a chance to observe genius at work: with infinite pains he tinkers with his phrases until they take on the unmistakable Beethoven sound and strength.

When he composed, his friends say, he was conscious of no one: he "muttered and howled"; he could be heard "singing, yelling, stamping his feet" in an "almost frightening performance." He would forget to eat.

In general Beethoven gave little attention to his daily life. His room was always a complete mess, full of heaps of dirty clothes, manuscripts, and dirty dishes. One visitor found a full chamberpot under the grand piano. Everything was dirty. He kept deciding to change his lodging: in 35 years he lived in 71 places. His servants never suited him, and never stayed long. From time to time he would grow suspicious of them, or of his friends, and accuse them of cheating him. Sensitive and quarrelsome, he was "up in arms at the most trifling fancied slight."

But it is easy to make Beethoven sound less sociable than he actually was. After an outburst of rage he would apologize the next day, and he was ready to help his former enemies in need. He enjoyed company: he once cooked dinner for a group of friends, who urged him to stick to composing. He liked to make good coffee for friends who visited him. He enjoyed making puns, often on people's names: his puns are terrible.

He got up early in the morning to work, then after breakfast liked to walk in the fields until afternoon, when he would go to one of Vienna's coffeehouses to read the paper and gossip. In summer he liked to move out of Vienna into the country. "Nature was like food to him, he seemed really to live in it," said a friend.

A visitor who met him in 1822 describes Beethoven: "His talk and his actions . . . all radiated a truly childlike amiability, carelessness, and confidence in everyone who approached him. Even his barking tirades—like that against his Viennese contemporaries, which I have already mentioned—are only explosions of his fanciful imagination and his momentary excitement. They are uttered without haughtiness, without any feeling of bitterness and hatefulness—and are simply blustered out lightly, good-humoredly. . . . To this we must add the most cheerful recognition of merit in others, if only it be distinctive and individual. (How he speaks of Handel, Bach, Mozart!) He does not, however, where his greater works are concerned, allow others to find fault (and who would have the right to do so?) yet he never actually overvalues them; and with regard to his lesser things is more inclined, perhaps, to abandon them with a laugh than any other person. He does this the more since once he is in the vein, rough, striking witticisms, droll conceits, surprising and exciting paradoxes suggest themselves to him in a continuous flow. Hence in all seriousness I claim that he even appears to be amiable. Or if you shrink from this word, I might say that the dark, unlicked bear seems so ingenuous and confiding, growls and shakes his shaggy pelt so harmlessly and grotesquely that it is a pleasure, and one has to be kind to him, even though he were nothing but a bear in fact and had done no more than a bear's best."

The great misfortune of Beethoven's life, which cut him off from his fellow men, accounted for many of his eccentricities. When he was 28 the first symptoms of deafness appeared—a humming and buzzing in his ears. Gradually this deafness increased, obscuring all sounds. Beethoven could not hear his works performed; he could not conduct, or perform as a soloist with an orchestra; his friends had to communicate with him by writing their remarks in the small notebook he carried. Beethoven's response, as always, was to fight. Occasionally he pitied himself: we have a letter he wrote in the summer of 1802 to his brothers. He never sent this letter, usually called the Heiligenstadt Testament; it was found among his possessions after his death.

"O my fellow men, who consider me, or describe me as unfriendly, peevish or even misanthropic, how greatly do you wrong me. For you do not know the secret reason why I appear to you to be so. Ever since my childhood my heart and soul have been imbued with the tender feeling of goodwill; and I have always been ready to perform even great actions. But just think, for the last six years I have been afflicted with an incurable complaint which has been made worse by incompetent doctors. From year to year my hopes of being cured have gradually been shattered and finally I have been forced to accept the prospect of a *permanent infirmity* (the curing of which may perhaps take years or may even prove to be impossible). . . . If at times I decided just to ignore my infirmity, alas! how cruelly was I then driven back by the intensified sad experience of my poor hearing. Yet I could not bring myself to say to people: 'Speak up, shout, for I am deaf." Alas! how could I possibly refer to the impairing *of a sense* which at one time I possessed in the greatest perfection, even to a degree of perfection such as assuredly few in my profession possess or have ever possessed—Oh, I cannot do it; so forgive me, if you ever see me withdrawing from your company which I used to enjoy. Moreover my misfortune pains me doubly, inasmuch as it leads to my being misjudged. For me there can be no relaxation in human society, no refined conversations, no mutual confidences. I must live quite alone and may creep into society only as often as sheer necessity demands: I must live like an outcast. If I appear in company I am overcome by a burning anxiety, a fear that I am running the risk of letting people notice my condition. . . . But how humiliated I have felt if somebody standing beside me heard the sound of a flute in the distance and *I heard nothing*, or if somebody heard *a shepherd sing* and again I heard nothing—Such experiences almost made me despair, and I was on the point of putting an end to my life—The only thing that held me back was *my art.* For indeed it seemed to me impossible to leave this world before I had produced all the works that I felt the urge to compose; and thus I have dragged on this miserable existence—a truly miserable existence . . . *Patience*—that is the virtue, I am told, which I must now choose for my guide; and I now possess it—I hope that I shall persist in my resolve to endure to the end. . . . At the early age of 28 I was obliged to become a philosopher, though this was not easy; for indeed this is more difficult for an artist than for anyone else—Almighty God, who look down into my innermost soul, you see into my heart, and you know that it is filled with love for humanity and a desire to do good. Of my fellow men, when someday you read this statement, remember that you have done me wrong; and let some unfortunate man derive comfort from the thought that he has found another equally unfortunate who, not withstanding all the obstacles imposed by nature, yet did everything in his power to be raised to the rank of noble artists and human beings."

In another letter Beethoven says, "Resignation, what a wretched resource! Yet it is all that is left to me." He defied life to defeat him: "I will seize Fate by the throat; it shall certainly not bend and crush me completely." He lived his life in this spirit, deferring to no man. Not for him a job as the servant of a nobleman: he treated noblemen as his equals if he respected them, and ignored the others. Nor did he cut himself off from loving people because of his deafness: we know he was in love, although we do not know the lady's name, and we know that when one of his brothers died, Beethoven took over responsibility for the raising of his nephew Karl, and gave him all his love. He managed the job poorly, having too much love and too little wisdom: the result was a great deal of grief for Beethoven.

But he rose above his suffering and defied it to create his major works. When his final illness came, Beethoven fought to live: he still had projects in mind. He died during a tremendous thunderstorm, March 16, 1827: friends report that during a thunderclap Beethoven raised himself on his bed, clenched his fist and brandished it at the sky, then fell back dead. It would have been in character. His contemporary, the Austrian poet Grillparzer spoke a funeral oration: "He . . . was possessed. Seeking one goal, caring only for one result, suffering and sacrificing for one purpose, thus did this man go through life."

CARL MARIA VON WEBER (1786-1826)

At one point in his career Carl Maria von Weber planned to write a guide to Europe for the traveling musician, which would tell all the things Weber had had to learn the hard way—how to get publicity for a concert, what hall to give it in, the quality of local musicians, and who to approach to hire them. By Weber's time there were enough traveling virtuosos to provide a market for such a book. Fewer musicians had permanent jobs with the church or a noble employer: more needed other ways of making money.

Sometime before the French Revolution began in 1789 a new attitude started to spread, which was to be called Romanticism: it influenced music, as well as the world in which the musicians worked. People rebelled against monarchs and a system in which the nobility had all the power and the money; nationalism developed as a strong force. Weber was consciously writing *German* opera and *German* music. Romantic artists tended to be multi-talented—Weber was a musician, writer, and artist—and they became stars in a way they had not been before. Audiences swooned over the great virtuosos, such as Liszt and Paganini. They loved the pale, handsome, sickly Weber as pianist and conductor. (Weber was one of the first great conductors: the idea that the conductor was the dictator of the orchestra first emerged in this period.) And Romanticism's pre-occupations provided new subjects for operas such as Weber's—the supernatural, national themes, the Orient, and the medieval world. Where Metastasian opera had demanded a happy ending with all reconciled to society's rules, opera now often took an interest in the outcast, the man who rebels against society's rules.

Weber came from a family of musical vagabonds whose lives would have appealed to Romantic artists as a good subject. His father Franz Anton (1734?-1812) was a man of many careers and talents, serving as a soldier, a steward, a musician, the manager of a traveling theatrical troupe, and a lithographer. His brother Fridolin's daughter married Mozart; somewhere in his wanderings Franz Anton became a self-made nobleman by adding the "von" to his name. His second wife, a pretty young singer, gave birth to Carl Maria, we think on November 18, 1786. He was a sickly, lame child, who may have inherited tuberculosis from his mother, who died when he was twelve. He grew up in various theatres of Germany, picking up an education along the way. One teacher was Michael Haydn.

Carl Maria showed musical talent young, singing beautifully, playing the piano well, and learning to compose early. At 13 he wrote an opera which got performed (he later said, "Puppies and first operas should be drowned."); at 16 he wrote a better one. Not yet 18, he got his first major job, conducting the orchestra at Breslau. In two difficult years he made many reforms. He overspent his income during a series of love affairs, nearly lost his life, and did lose his singing voice: his father, who was now working with lithography, an art Carl Maria had also tried, left some acid on the table in a wine bottle. Carl Maria, entering the room, took a swig. During his illness, all his reforms were undone. He resigned.

The Webers now spent some time in Wurtemburg as the guests of the king's brother, Duke of Wurtemburg. The gluttonous ruler, who was so fat he had to cut a section out of his table to get within arm's reach, disliked Weber, and the feeling was returned. When Carl Maria's father, now senile, paid his own debts with money of the duke's which had been entrusted to Carl Maria, the king had Carl Maria charged with theft and embezzlement. He was acquitted, but was required to come to an agreement with his 42 creditors to pay off his debts gradually and was banished from the country in 1810.

After this frightening experience Weber and his music became more mature. In 1813 he was called to Prague to become Director of the Opera, and he spent three busy very years reorganizing the house, learning Czech, and having an affair with an older singer. He produced 62 operas and became friendly with a younger singer he had hired, Caroline Brandt, to whom he eventually proposed. She did not want to give up her singing career, but Weber said, "My wife must belong to me, not to the world; I must be able to support her without a struggle." Being as dictatorial as the next conductor, he got his way.

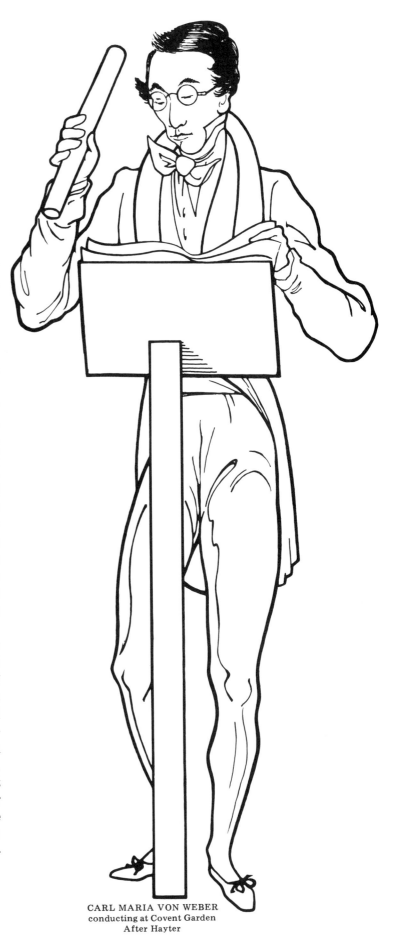

CARL MARIA VON WEBER
conducting at Covent Garden
After Hayter

In 1816 Weber accepted an offer to become the Royal Saxon *Kapellmeister* in Dresden, a sleepy backwater of a town. The king distrusted Weber for having written German patriotic music, and preferred Italian composers anyhow. His Italian *Kapellmeister*, Morlacchi, got the lion's share of the budget, the vacations, and the singers; Weber got more of the work. A great deal of his time was wasted writing the obligatory cantatas setting vapid poetry to celebrate royal birthdays, weddings, and christenings.

But Weber found time to write an opera, *Der Freischütz*, which opened in Berlin June 18, 1821, and triumphed all over Germany as the first great German Romantic opera, with a German story and a German style. The lovely music carried the rather foolish story. Debussy said of the orchestration, "He scrutinizes the soul of each instrument and exposes it with a gentle hand."

After this success, Weber made a concert tour of Germany and Denmark, then returned to boring Dresden to write a cantata for the king's sister's birthday. The king refused him permission to produce *Die Drei Pintos*, the comic opera on which he was working. Discouraged, he put it aside: it remained a series of sketches, later deciphered and completed by young Gustav Mahler. At this moment of depression Weber suffered his first tubercular hemorrhage: the rest of his work was produced in a race with death.

After the success of *Freischütz* Rossini's friend the impresario Domenico Barbaja commissioned Weber to write a grand opera for Vienna. He was eager to do so, but had no libretto. Helmina von Chezy, an incompetent local poetess, patched together a silly story about medieval Europe—*Euryanthe*, produced in Vienna in 1823. Schumann said of it, "This music is as yet far too little known and recognized. It is heart's blood, the noblest he had; the opera cost him part of his life—truly. But it has also made him immortal."

By now Weber knew that he had not long to live, and worried a great deal about providing for his wife and children. He received an offer to compose and conduct an opera for Drury Lane Theatre in England: his doctor told him if he stopped work and moved to Italy, he might live another six years, but if he went to England he could hardly survive six months. Weber decided that he must take the offer in the hopes of making a fortune for his family, instead of living on, unable to make any income. After setting a wretched libretto called *Oberon*, Weber left for England, saying, "I'm going to London to die."

In London he was lionized: everyone knew *Freischütz*, and everyone admired his conducting. Weber had become one of the great conductors of the age. Someone describes him as he led the orchestra with a scroll of rolled paper (the baton was not used yet): "In conducting Weber became so moved and excited that he stood as if transfigured and often seemed to be making music with his whole face."

Oberon succeeded: Weber conducted, though his lungs were so nearly gone that he was hardly able to breathe any more. He wrote brave letters to Caroline, despite his terrible homesickness, and hoped only that he could live long enough to see his family again. Characteristically, however, he conducted an extra performance to aid a charity. He grew weaker and weaker, still was determined to return to Dresden. But on the morning of June 5 he was found dead in bed, with all his effects neatly in order to give as little trouble as possible to his hosts. He was buried in London: in 1844 his successor as *Kapellmeister* in Dresden, Richard Wagner, who as a boy had been inspired by Weber's conducting, raised money to return the body to Germany. So ends the too-brief story of Weber, whom Stravinsky called "that prince of music."

GIOACCHINO ROSSINI
1792-1868

"If theatre is an insane asylum," Rossini is supposed to have said, "then opera is the ward for incurables." Working in the insane world of opera brought him from obscurity to fame, but the working conditions nearly killed him.

Born February 29, 1792 in Pesaro, a small Italian town ruled by the Pope, Gioacchino Rossini was the only child of the town trumpeter and inspector of slaughter-houses and a baker's daughter who was a good soprano and sang occasionally in the opera. Rossini said, "She sang all the time, even when doing household chores. . . Her naturally expressive voice was beautiful and full of grace—sweet, like her appearance."

Young Rossini learned music informally until he went to the *Liceo Musicale* at Bologna in 1804. In 1805, while playing in the theatre's pit orchestra, Rossini attracted the attention of a Venetian impresario whose company was performing there. When the soprano made dreadful noises during a cadenza, Rossini went into gales of laughter. The angry impresario was disarmed by his charm and talent. When Rossini was forced by poverty to leave the school in 1810, this man gave him a one-act libretto to set. After *La Cambiale di matrimonio* was performed successfully in November 1810, Rossini's career was launched. Before he was twenty-one, he became one of the most sought-after composers of the day.

ROSSINI after E. Carjat, 1856

His life was hectic and exciting. Arriving in a new town, where the impresario had a contract with him, he would be given a libretto, or part of it: often he did not know the end of the story when he composed the beginning. Not knowing the ending often made no difference, as the story was senseless anyhow—just an excuse for singers to be emotional all over the stage. Rossini once boasted, "Give me a laundry list and I'll set it to music." He wrote at great speed, working with people talking around him, distracted only by frequent love affairs: women chased the handsome and famous young composer, which was fortunate as he was too busy and too lazy to chase them. (Rossini was famous for being lazy: people claimed that once, when he was composing in bed and an aria dropped to the floor, he was too lazy to pick it up, and wrote another instead.)

How could a composer write operas fast enough to turn out thirty in ten years? To begin with, as an opera written for one town would not have been heard in another, Rossini economically recycled material from old works in composing new ones (most composers did this until modern communications destroyed the decent obscurity of a composer's minor works). The overture to *The Barber of Seville* had served three previous operas. But Rossini could also be fast and good at once: he wrote *The Barber* in thirteen days.

To work at this speed a composer had to take pressure well. Rossini once advised another composer, "Wait until the evening before the opening night [to write the overture]. Nothing primes inspiration more than necessity, whether it be the presence of a copyist waiting for your work, or the prodding of an impresario tearing his hair. In my time, all the impresarios of Italy were bald at thirty . . . I wrote the overture of *La Gazza Ladra* the day of its opening in the theatre itself, where I was imprisoned by the director and under the surveillance of the stagehands, who were instructed to throw my original text through the window, page by page, to the copyists waiting below to transcribe it. In default of pages, they were ordered to throw me out the window bodily."

A composer also had to take either success or failure in stride. After one disaster Rossini sent home to mama merely a drawing of a little glass bottle—a *fiasco*. When *The Barber of Seville* opened in Rome February 20, 1816, with Rossini conducting, the audience laughed a lot, but not at the opera: a singer developed a nosebleed on stage which couldn't be stopped; a cat came on stage and took part in the finale. Rossini stayed home in bed the next night. He was awakened by the sound of a mob approaching, and thought at first that the audience had decided to exterminate the composer; instead, the work had triumphed, and the audience had come to cheer him.

Rossini's early operas had not made him rich: for the first nine he earned about $1650 total. *The Barber* was the seventeenth of his thirty-nine: for it he got about $1400 and a brown suit with gilt buttons, about a third as much as one of the leading singers got. But now he worked for several years with a man who helped make him rich, Domenico Barbaja, an illiterate former cafe waiter in Naples, who had risen, through owning a gambling house, to become the man in charge of all the Neapolitan theatres, which all had gambling tables. Barbaja's leading soprano, the great dramatic singer Isabella Colbran, was his mistress. Rossini signed a contract with Barbaja to direct the San Carlo Theatre in Naples, for which he was to write two operas a year. He got a fee, and a percentage of the gambling profits.

After writing a series of tragic operas for Colbran, Rossini married her in 1822; she was thirty-seven, and quite wealthy. Barbaja, who remained their friend, organized a Rossini festival in Vienna for them. The city was gripped by a Rossini fever. Salieri arranged for Rossini to meet Beethoven, whose works Rossini admired. In

1860 in Paris Rossini described this meeting to
Wagner. No picture, Rossini said, expressed
"the indefinable sadness spread across
all his features, so that from under

ROSSINI after Mailly.

heavy eyebrows there shone, as if from the depths of caverns, two eyes which, though small, seemed to pierce you. The voice was soft and slightly fogged." Beethoven praised *The Barber*, saying, "It will be played as long as Italian opera exists."

Rossini was now an international celebrity. After the success in Venice of *Semiramide* he was escorted home triumphantly by a fleet of gondolas. In one visit to England he made 40,000 pounds, while Colbran made even more for singing—an immense fortune for those days. The Rossinis settled in Paris, where the government made Rossini head of a major theatre, and the press reported his doings as if he were a visiting head of state. The government gave him an annual pension of $15,000, and he began making French versions of his operas, as Gluck had done before him.

But problems began to close in upon him, and the years of working at top speed took their toll. Colbran's voice was failing, and she became extravagant, quarrelsome, and addicted to gambling. Eventually the pair separated. The death of Rossini's mother in February, 1827 crushed him: he had always remained close to his parents, and now felt he no longer had anyone to whom to bring home his successes. He talked of writing one more grand opera, then retiring. *William Tell*, performed in October, 1829, was indeed his last opera.

A long period of ill health followed. Olympe Pelissier, who came into his life as a nurse, became his protector and mistress, and eventually, after Colbran's death in 1845, his second wife. An intelligent woman, she was kind, cheerful, and witty, and shared one of Rossini's major interests—food. She once said, "the Maestro and I live to eat ... and we acquit ourselves of this duty religiously," and described herself as "a fat woman who is occupied from morning to evening with digesting." Rossini himself cooked, as well as being a serious eater. A grocer who had just been crossexamined by the master about his stock of pasta was told that his customer was a great composer; "If he knows as much about music as he does about macaroni, he must write beautiful stuff."

But between 1830 and 1855 Rossini's health kept him from working and even from eating. Several times he was near death; but after 1855 he had a final period of health and happiness. He and Olympe returned to Paris from Italy, and summered at a villa in Passy, wintered in Paris. In 1857 Rossini began composing again—principally small pieces for their famous Saturday evening receptions; famous men of the world fought to be invited. A musical entertainment was presented, often with one of the witty little piano pieces Rossini was writing, which he called "Sins of My Old Age." They had curious titles—"Pretentious Prelude," "Asthmatic Etude," "Limping Waltz," "Convulsive Prelude," or "Four hors d'oeuvres: radishes, theme and variations on anchovies, gherkins, butter." People urged him to write another opera, but Rossini said, "I no longer compose, being at the age at which one, rather, decomposes." He once boasted, "Retiring in time takes genius, too."

His last major work was a mass, which he called "little solemn mass" and scored for small forces. His preface addresses God: "Dear God, here is this poor little Mass, finished at last. Have I written truly sacred music, or just damned bad music? [A French pun] Thou knowest I was born for comic opera! Not much skill, but quite a bit of feeling—that's how I'd sum it up. Blessed be Thy Name, and grant me Paradise!" Like all Rossini's music, the piece has great charm.

Rossini died November 13, 1868: he left his money to establish a music school in his native city, Rossini Prizes for French singers, and a home for old opera singers in Paris: his sharp wit had often concealed his kind-heartedness.

After a drawing by Franz von Schober.

Michael Vogl leading his friend Franz Schubert

FRANZ SCHUBERT (1797-1828)

He was a short man, just under five foot two, a bit too plump: his friends called him *"Schwammerl"* ("Tubby"). One says he had "a round, fat face, short neck, a not very high forehead, and thick, brown, naturally curly hair. . . . His head sat somewhat squeezed between his shoulders, inclining rather forward. Schubert always wore spectacles. . . . He was only really animated among intimate friends. . . . Shy and taciturn, especially in smart society, which he only frequented in order to accompany his songs, more or less as a favor."

Schubert's personality is less clear to us than that of most composers. His real life was led in his music. Yet he was the center of a group of friends who cared for him as a person as well as a composer. Apparently he had charm, a quality which evaporates from descriptions: all we have left are the bare facts of his short life, and his music.

He was born January 31, 1797, one of the many children of a Viennese schoolmaster. The family liked music: eventually young Franz played viola in a family quartet, with papa the cellist, and brothers Ferdinand and Ignaz the violinists. In October 1808, Franz was taken into the choir of the Imperial Court Chapel, where he got a very good musical training. He conducted the student orchestra and did some composing, with Antonio Salieri, Mozart's old nemesis, as one of his teachers. At 16 he wrote his first symphony; the next year he wrote his first great song.

His school friend Josef von Spaun, who bought for Schubert the music paper he could not afford himself, describes watching Schubert write one of his great songs, in 1815: "we found Schubert all aglow, reading Goethe's "The *Erlkönig*" (Elfking) aloud from the book. He paced up and down several times with the book, suddenly he sat down and in no time at all (just as quickly as one can write) there was the glorious ballad finished on paper. We ran with it to the Seminary, for there was no pianoforte at Schubert's, and there, on the very same evening, 'The *Erlkönig*' was sung and enthusiastically received."

Apparently Schubert usually composed this way—with great speed, and entirely in his head. Someone once gave him a poem just written. He took it over to the window, read it through a few times, then said, "I've got it already, it's done, and it's going to be quite good." These songs tossed off so easily express the soul of the poem he set.

From 1813 on, while continuing his lessons with Salieri, Schubert was training to be a teacher. His father felt that a career in music could not be relied upon for support. Schubert taught a while, then stopped in 1817: apparently he was a poor disciplinarian. From this time on he usually lived in the apartment of one or another kind friend, and composed. "It was interesting to see him compose. He very seldom made use of the pianoforte while doing it. He often used to say it would make him lose his train of thought. Quite quietly, and hardly disturbed by the unavoidable chatter and din of his friends around him, he would sit at the little writing table, bent over the music paper and the book of poems (he was short-sighted), bite his pen, drum with his fingers at the same time, trying things out, and continue to write easily and fluently, without many corrections, as if it had to be like that and not otherwise."

At this time an important figure came into Schubert's life—Michael Vogl, a baritone with a great reputation, 30 years older than Schubert. Vogl's voice was beginning to go, but he was an intelligent singer with a real love of music; quickly he recognized how marvellous these songs his small shy friend wrote were. He took

FRANZ SCHUBERT from a drawing by Moritz von Schwind, 1825.

Schubert under his protection—the two of them looked funny together, as the caricature shows—and performed his songs everywhere. Often Schubert's friends would arrange what they called "Schubertiads"—private concerts at the homes of music-loving friends, where nothing was played but Schubert's music. Those who loved music were eager to be there. Of course, Schubert made no money from these.

Few of the usual sources of income were open to him. He was not a virtuoso performer on any instrument. He applied for minor jobs assisting *kapellmeisters*, but no one had heard of him, and his letters were lost. He did begin selling pieces— mostly songs—to publishers in 1821, and had published up to Opus 100 by the time of his death, but made little money in exchange. Most of his instrumental music was not published in his lifetime. Schubert tried another traditional route to fame and fortune—writing opera. But Vienna was in the grip of a Rossini fever and didn't want German operas. While several of Schubert's were performed, they were handicapped by having laughable librettos.

Schubert's unbusinesslike ways helped keep him poor. He really wasn't very interested in money, and he often mislaid his manuscripts: if he lost the piece on which he was working, he could always write something else. A number of pieces ended up "unfinished" because he lost track of them. In the fifty years after his death scholars engaged in one of the great treasure hunts of history looking for Schubert manuscripts. In 1838 Robert Schumann found Schubert's Ninth Symphony, which had never been played, in the possession of Ferdinand Schubert. Wildly excited Schumann wrote Clara, "It is not possible to describe it to you. All the instruments are human voices. It is gifted beyond measure." Mendelssohn conducted the premiere in Leipzig in 1839: Schumann's review said, "It bears within the core of everlasting youth."

In 1822 Schubert was dangerously ill. His hair fell out, and he never entirely recovered his health. But he continued to pour out great music. He became more solitary than ever: although he greatly admired Beethoven's music, and although Beethoven, who kept track of other composers, praised Schubert's works, Schubert was too shy to try to meet Beethoven. But he carried a torch at Beethoven's funeral, to honor him.

Schubert's district of Vienna had infected water; his health already weakened, Schubert developed typhoid. He died November 20, 1828, only 31, and was buried near Beethoven.

All his music was early music: we cannot know where his genius would have taken him. The poet Grillparzer said everything in his epitaph: "THE ART OF MUSIC HERE ENTOMBED A RICH POSSESSION, BUT EVEN FAIRER HOPES."

HECTOR BERLIOZ (1803-1869)

Berlioz once said, "I took up music where Beethoven left it"; he seems also to have taken up Beethoven's struggle against a life full of pain and griefs. Berlioz was full of optimism, tremendous aspirations, and insatiable openness to experience. "Despite all my efforts, life escapes me, I only catch shreds of it," he once wrote. Like Beethoven he refused to accept defeat: "I defy them to wear me down."

The greatest French composer, critic, and conductor of his century was born December 11, 1803, in La Côte Saint-André, a very small town in southern France where his father was the local doctor. Unlike most great composers, Berlioz had little exposure to music as a child, was not a prodigy, and never became a virtuoso

HECTOR BERLIOZ after Carjat, 1857.

on any instrument. He wanted to study music; his father sent him to Paris to study medicine. Berlioz took one look at the corpse he was expected to dissect, jumped out the window, and went to enroll at the Conservatoire: he would become a composer.

His teachers found him stubbornly set on his own ideas—which they pronounced unplayable. The young man made himself known as a character in Paris by assigning himself the duty of protecting masterworks of opera from the "improvements" of conductors. In his marvellous *Memoirs*, Berlioz describes a performance at the Opéra in which the conductor had dared rescore an opera by Berlioz's idol Gluck. "Although boiling with rage, I managed to restrain myself until the end of the aria; then in the short pause that followed, I shouted, 'Gluck put no cymbals there; who has dared to correct Gluck?'" Once he provoked a riot. An audience member who saw Berlioz on such an occasion describes "a young man trembling with indignation, his hands clenched, his eyes flashing, and with a huge head of hair—such a head of hair. It looked like an enormous umbrella of hair, projecting like a canopy over the beak of a bird of prey."

A master of instrumentation and the writer of one of the first books on orchestration, Berlioz took such matters seriously; he was among the first musicians to believe that works of earlier composers should be played as written, not rescored to suit the taste of the moment. He greeted the corruption of works by his favorite composers with fierce indignation: Schumann once said, "Berlioz does not try to be pleasing and elegant. What he hates, he grasps fiercely by the hair; what he loves, he almost crushes in his fervor."

Berlioz was passionate about everything, not just music. He seems to have had stronger powers of response than most of us, and responded to many things with a violence which frightened others. Late in life, while rereading his beloved Shakespeare and Virgil in preparing the libretto for his gigantic opera *Les Troyens*, Berlioz commented, "I feel that my heart will burst when I come across lines like that."

Literature led him to one of his volcanic loves. In 1827 Harriet Smithson, an English actress, appeared in Paris in the first productions of Shakespeare seen there. Berlioz saw her as Ophelia and Juliet and fell violently in love with Harriet and Shakespeare simultaneously. His wild letters frightened her; he pursued her in vain, decided she was worthless, wrote a symphony in which she figured as a witch, and fell in love with another woman who, while Berlioz was studying in Rome, married a wealthy older man. Berlioz, enraged, left Rome, taking with him pistols and poison: he intended to kill his faithless love, her husband, and her mother, whom he blamed for the treachery. He paused long enough to finish orchestrating the piece he was writing. He got as far as Nice, paused because he was hungry, tried to commit suicide, failed, ran out of anger, and remained there for three happy weeks, writing an overture.

When he returned to Paris, he returned to loving Harriet. After major traumas, including another suicide attempt, he ultimately married her, and they lived together quite unhappily. Her acting was no longer successful; she became an alcoholic. Berlioz, unable to bear her jealousy, slovenliness, and quarrelsomeness, moved out and took a mistress. Harriet became ill, and needed nursing day and night for some years. Berlioz provided this, and often attended her himself. To earn the money he needed, he continued expending his energy as a music critic—a job he called "my life sentence of hard labor."

When Harriet died, he reflected that there was "nothing left" between them: "We each suffered so much at the other's hands." "How horrible life is. Everything

comes back to me ... her great qualities, her cruel demands, her injustice, and her genius and her woes ... She made me understand Shakespeare and true dramatic art." The same man who had such volcanic passions amazes us by his power to detach himself from them and observe with great accuracy and detachment. This quality made him a wonderful critic and a very fine autobiographer: it also made him a great conductor and musical educator. When he wrote passionate new pieces, revolutionary in style, Berlioz could not get them performed. Coolly he organized concerts. Conductors ruined his works at these concerts. Coolly he became a conductor himself, one of the best of the period. The critics misunderstood his works. He became a critic as well as a composer, conductor, and concert-organizer, and spent a large part of his life educating the public in the new music.

He could be devastating in reviewing shoddy music: speaking of a work by Clapisson, he observed, "You will wonder how grossness can combine with flatness. I do not know how the composer did it; it is one of his trade secrets." But he was enthusiastic about the best of his contemporaries, and always responsive to good work. One has to love a man who, late in life, after serving on a jury which awarded a prize to his young friend Camille Saint-Saens, ran down the street to be the first to bring Saint-Saens the news.

Throughout his life he was loved strongly by a few friends, and appreciated by the best judges. Dramatic events marked his life: at one moment of despair, he was saved by a gift of 20,000 francs from the incredible violin virtuoso Niccolo Paganini (1782-1840), who hailed him as a successor to Beethoven. The gift allowed him to take off from his criticism to finish the large dramatic symphony, *Romeo et Juliette*.

Berlioz's conceptions led him onward to larger and larger works, anticipating those of Wagner, Mahler and other composers of the century. He was never afraid of an idea because of its scale: he once started to write an opera about The Day of Judgement.

PAGANINI in London, 1851.

His enemies complained that he was overly dramatic, but he did not choose to suffer the dramatic tragedies which marked his life: in 1867, for example, as friends were taking him to a party in his honor, the news was brought to Berlioz of the death of his adored only child Louis. The great novelist Flaubert once said that when one knew Berlioz's life, one could no longer complain of one's own.

In his last years Berlioz could no longer fight against the ignorance and indifference that met his works. "I desire only sleep while awaiting something more permanent," he said. He could not get his masterpiece *Les Troyens* performed: "I would rather be stabbed ten times in the chest with a dirty kitchen-knife than to hear anyone mangle the last monologue of the Queen of Carthage," he wrote, rejecting a proposal for an inadequate production. Finally he wrote, "Everything comes to him who waits; if we would only live to be 200, if we could stay young, intelligent, and strong during that couple of centuries, we men of ideas—men of fixed ideas, occasionally; and if meanwhile the others died at 30 or 40 no cleverer than they were at birth—then, then, the obstacles in our path would be child's play."

FELIX MENDELSSOHN (1809-1847)

All his life long Felix Mendelssohn was as hard-working and self-controlled as his family had taught him to be. The Mendelssohns were fascinating and talented: grandfather Moses (1729-1786) had started life as a hunchbacked poor boy in a ghetto, and through his determination and brilliance had become well-to-do and a major philosopher, a symbol of the brotherhood of all men at a time when, as a Jew, if he walked with his children through the streets of Berlin, they were occasionally stoned. Felix's father Abraham (1776-1835) was a banker, a good man who made a fortune honestly in a troubled period. While his children were young, Abraham had his family become Christians: he saw conversion as "the admission ticket to European culture."

His oldest child, Fanny, born in 1805, was a musical prodigy; but then so was his second, Felix, born February 3, 1809. The two were always extremely close through life. Felix, who was a very good pianist, asserted that Fanny was even better; but Abraham objected strongly to the idea of his daughter having a career so she was never able to use her musical talent. She composed well too. Felix published some of her songs under his own name: when anyone praised them, he took great pleasure in telling their real authorship. When Fanny was married, she composed her own wedding music.

Abraham worked his four children very hard: they had to learn music, Latin, Greek, mathematics, history, geography, esthetics, politics, German, foreign literature, art, French, English, and Italian. Sundays were holidays, with an extra hour's sleep—till 6. This training produced children with a wide cultural background, and well-developed talents. Felix drew well, and wrote good letters. He was practically a perfect boy—polite, self-controlled, even-tempered, kindly, and handsome.

He also had a major musical talent. His father trained him well, if with conservative tastes: Abraham revered Bach and was suspicious of Beethoven's music. From the age of 11 Felix was composing copiously: occasionally papa hired an orchestra for him to conduct, so that he could try out his pieces. Before long he was composing great music: at 16 he produced a lovely Octet—"I had a beautiful time writing it," he said; next year he wrote *The Midsummer Night's Dream Overture*, for his favorite Shakespeare play. In 1829 Felix did something which had been regarded as impossible: he trained the singers and conducted them in the first performance of Bach's *St. Matthew Passion* since Bach's death. Fanny sang in the chorus, and was extremely proud.

Felix then toured Europe, much of which he'd already seen. England became his second home: the English were at ease with a composer who was always a gentleman, and Mendelssohn loved them as much as they loved him. Later, he became a welcome guest of Queen Victoria and Prince Albert, who would sing duets with him: when the Queen asked what favor she could do for Mendelssohn, he asked to be shown the royal nurseries. He was always tactful.

He had a few reservations about the English, however: like many Germans, he felt the English did not appreciate Shakespeare as well as the Germans, and when he toured Scotland and the Hebrides he hated the folk songs and the bagpipes.

In Rome, Mendelssohn met Berlioz, there on scholarship. They became friends, although Mendelssohn disliked Berlioz' music. Berlioz said, "He has an enormous, extraordinary, prodigious talent." Mendelssohn wrote home, "His instrumentation is terribly dirty. One feels like washing his hands after handling one of

FELIX MENDELSSOHN-BARTHOLDY after J. W. Childe, 1829. Berlin.

his scores." One of Mendelssohn's least agreeable traits is a tendency to condescend to others, particularly those whom he felt weren't quite as gentlemanly as himself: Berlioz was too wild, Schumann too extravagant . . . The composers he liked best were polite, genteel second-raters, like Sterndale Bennett (an Englishman).

When Mendelssohn returned to Berlin in 1832, his family wanted him to become conductor of the *Singakademie* in succession to his old teacher. After a long, bitter campaign, Mendelssohn lost the election for the post—too young. He and his family were very bitter: Mendelssohn didn't really like to fight—it was undignified—but hated to lose, and bore grudges. He never quite forgave a bad review, and tended to faint when crossed or defeated. I think perhaps he had been trained to control himself so rigidly that he could not admit to having the emotions of anger or frustration everyone experiences in life.

Mendelssohn conducted the Düsseldorf Rhenish Music Festival, very successfully; he was then called to head the famous Leipzig *Gewandhaus* Orchestra in Bach's city. He increased the size of the orchestra, got the musicians better salaries and a pension fund, and became known as the greatest conductor of Europe. He and Berlioz were among the first to use the baton. Mendelssohn was incessantly active as a conductor, music director, teacher, performer, entrepreneur, and composer. His leisure time was filled with traveling, hiking, collecting, and musical scholarship: Sir George Grove wrote, "We may almost be pardoned for wondering how he can have found time to write any music at all."

The death of Mendelssohn's father in 1835 affected him strongly: they had been close. Fanny told him he should marry. He picked a nineteen-year-old girl out of a chorus he conducted: Cecile Jeanrenaud was a pretty, sensible, soothing, dull girl. Felix went off for a month to decide whether marrying her would be sensible, then proposed. They married in 1837, and lived cosily ever afterwards, with five children.

In 1840 Felix was called to Berlin by the new King of Prussia, who wanted to make Berlin an international center of the arts. He gave Mendelssohn a job with a large title and powers which Mendelssohn was unable to get defined. Occasionally he was asked to compose something to order, but he wrote very little in this frustrating period of nearly five years. He continued traveling all over Europe to conduct, but grew more doubtful of the music he was composing, slowly, with infinite revisions. He talked of "my dreadful disease" of revising.

After returning from a very tiring trip to England, Mendelssohn was greeted with the news that Fanny had died suddenly May 14, 1847. He collapsed totally. The closest emotional tie of his life was broken: "With her kindness and love she was part of myself every moment of my life. There was no joy I experienced without thinking of the joy she would feel with me." He was taken off to Switzerland, but could not recover any desire to live: asked how he felt, he replied, "Gray on gray." After a seizure in late October, he lost consciousness: in delirium he spoke only English. He died November 4, 1847.

Perhaps the most popular composer of his century, he was deeply mourned. Brahms hailed him as "the last of the great masters." As time passed, many felt he was a prodigy who had never quite fulfilled his promise, a conservative who had looked backward to the classical composers instead of seeing music's future. Pablo Casals described him as "a romantic who felt at ease within the mold of classicism"—not a bad thing to be. But one can't help wondering whether if he hadn't been so polite, so gentlemanly, so self-controlled, such a good boy, his talent might have developed further.